# Hokusai
## Birds, Flowers, and Nature
### COLORING BOOK

The Japanese woodblock artist Katsushika Hokusai, who lived from 1760 to 1849, had a great influence on many European artists, in particular, the Impressionist painters Claude Monet and Pierre-Auguste Renoir. Hokusai started sketching when he was five or six years old, and he became an apprentice wood engraver at the age of fourteen. At eighteen, he went to work in a master artist's studio, and a year later he published his first prints. Even though Hokusai had a very long career as an artist, he wrote that it wasn't until the age of seventy-two that he "finally apprehended something of the true quality of birds, animals, insects, fish, and of the vital nature of grasses and trees."

The woodblocks included in this coloring book are mostly from two untitled series of Hokusai's prints called Large Flowers and Small Flowers. They were created by carving a separate woodblock for every color and then printing them on top of each other to create a single complete image.

When you color the images, try to imagine the temperature and moisture in the air, the smell of the flowers, and the sounds of the birds. These are the things Hokusai tried to express, even though they are invisible. The 22 woodblock prints in this coloring book are shown as small pictures on the inside front and back covers. You might want to copy their original colors or you might decide to use your own. We've left the last page of this book blank so that you can draw and color a picture of your own.

mfa
BOSTON

Pomegranate kids

All works of art are from the collection of the Museum of Fine Arts, Boston. All are ink and color on paper and unless otherwise stated are *nishiki-e* woodblock prints.

1. *Shrike and Blessed Thistle (Mozu, oniazami),* from an untitled series known as Small Flowers, Edo period, about 1834. Vertical chūban; 25.5 x 18.8 cm (10 1/16 x 7 3/8 in.). William S. and John T. Spaulding Collection, 21.10226.

2. *Carp and Iris,* Edo period. Cut from horizontal aiban sheet; 23.4 x 29.5 cm (9 3/16 x 11 5/8 in.). William Sturgis Bigelow Collection, 11.20430.

3. *Kingfisher with Iris and Wild Pinks (Kawasemi, shaga, nadeshiko),* from an untitled series known as Small Flowers, Edo period, about 1834. Vertical chūban; 25.8 x 18.7 cm (10 3/16 x 7 3/8 in.). William S. and John T. Spaulding Collection, 21.10221.

4. *Chrysanthemums and Horsefly,* from an untitled series known as Large Flowers, Edo period, about 1833–1834. Horizontal ōban; 25.3 x 37 cm (9 15/16 x 14 9/16 in.). William S. and John T. Spaulding Collection, 21.6681.

5. *Hawfinch and Marvel-of-Peru (Ikaru, oshiroi no hana),* from an untitled series known as Small Flowers, Edo period, about 1834. Vertical chūban; 24.1 x 19 cm (9 1/2 x 7 1/2 in.). William Sturgis Bigelow Collection, 11.23024.

6. *Peonies and Canary (Shakuyaku, kanaari),* from an untitled series known as Small Flowers, Edo period, about 1834. Vertical chūban; 26 x 19.2 cm (10 1/4 x 7 9/16 in.). William S. and John T. Spaulding Collection, 21.10228.

7. *Peonies and Butterfly,* from an untitled series known as Large Flowers, Edo period, about 1833–1834. Horizontal ōban; 26.3 x 39 cm (10 3/8 x 15 3/8 in.). William Sturgis Bigelow Collection, 11.17593.

8. *Shrike and Bluebird with Begonia and Wild Strawberry (Mozu, ruri, yuki-no-shita, hebi-ichigo),* from the untitled series known as Small Flowers, Edo period, about 1834. Vertical chūban; 25.8 x 18.8 cm (10 3/16 x 7 3/8 in.). William S. and John T. Spaulding Collection, 21.10227.

9. *Grasshopper and Persimmon,* Edo period. Woodblock print (*surimono*); shikishiban; 21 x 18.4 cm (8 1/4 x 7 1/4 in.). William Sturgis Bigelow Collection, 11.25209.

10. *Hydrangeas and Swallow,* from an untitled series known as Large Flowers, Edo period, about 1833–1834. Horizontal ōban; 26.2 x 38.1 cm (10 5/16 x 15 in.). William Sturgis Bigelow Collection, 11.17592.

11. *Turtles and Reflected Plum Branch* (detail), Edo period, about 1795–1812. Woodblock print (*surimono*); ebangire; 18.6 x 51.8 cm (7 5/16 x 20 3/8 in.). William S. and John T. Spaulding Collection, 21.7866.

12. *Hawk and Cherry Blossoms* (detail), Edo period, about 1834. Vertical nagaban; 52.9 x 23.5 cm (20 13/16 x 9 1/4 in.). William Sturgis Bigelow Collection, 11.19656.

13. *Java Sparrow on Magnolia (Banchō, kobushi no hana),* from an untitled series known as Small Flowers, Edo period, about 1834. Vertical chūban; 24 x 18.8 cm (9 7/16 x 7 3/8 in.). William Sturgis Bigelow Collection, 11.25142.

14. *Lilies,* from an untitled series known as Large Flowers, Edo period, about 1833–1834. Horizontal ōban; 26.3 x 38.2 cm (10 3/8 x 15 1/16 in.). William Sturgis Bigelow Collection, 11.17598.

15. *Bullfinch and Weeping Cherry (Uso, shidarezakura),* from an untitled series known as Small Flowers, Edo period, about 1834. Vertical chūban; 25.5 x 18.7 cm (10 1/16 x 7 3/8 in.). William S. and John T. Spaulding Collection, 21.10229.

16. *Poppies,* from an untitled series known as Large Flowers, Edo period, about 1833–1834. Horizontal ōban; 26.2 x 38.4 cm (10 5/16 x 15 1/8 in.). William Sturgis Bigelow Collection, 11.17594.

17. *Hibiscus and Sparrow,* from an untitled series known as Large Flowers, Edo period, about 1833–1834. Horizontal ōban; 26.1 x 38.4 cm (10 1/4 x 15 1/8 in.). William Sturgis Bigelow Collection, 11.17595.

18. *Warbler and Roses (Kōchō, bara),* from an untitled series known as Small Flowers, Edo period, about 1834. Vertical chūban; 25.6 x 18.5 cm (10 1/16 x 7 5/16 in.). William S. and John T. Spaulding Collection, 21.10223.

19. *Bellflower and Dragonfly,* from an untitled series known as Large Flowers, Edo period, about 1833–1834. Horizontal ōban; 26.6 x 39.4 cm (10 1/2 x 15 1/2 in.). William S. and John T. Spaulding Collection, 21.6680.

20. *Wisteria and Wagtail (Fuji, sekirei),* from an untitled series known as Small Flowers, Edo period, about 1834. Vertical chūban; 25.7 x 18.7 cm (10 1/8 x 7 3/8 in.). William S. and John T. Spaulding Collection, 21.10219.

21. *Morning Glories and Tree Frog,* from an untitled series known as Large Flowers, Edo period, about 1833–1834. Horizontal ōban; 26.7 x 39 cm (10 1/2 x 15 3/8 in.). William Sturgis Bigelow Collection, 11.17596.

22. *Cuckoo and Azaleas (Hototogisu, satsuki),* from an untitled series known as Small Flowers, Edo period, about 1834. Vertical chūban; 24.1 x 19 cm (9 1/2 x 7 1/2 in.). William Sturgis Bigelow Collection, 11.23023.

Pomegranate Communications, Inc.
Box 808022, Petaluma CA 94975
800 227 1428   www.pomegranate.com

© 2010 Museum of Fine Arts, Boston
Line drawings © Pomegranate Communications, Inc.

Catalog No. CB121
Designed and rendered by Susan Koop
Printed in Korea
21 20 19 18 17 16 15 14 13 12     10 9 8 7 6 5 4 3 2

Distributed by Pomegranate Europe Ltd.
Unit 1, Heathcote Business Centre, Hurlbutt Road
Warwick, Warwickshire CV34 6TD, UK
[+44] 0 1926 430111
sales@pomeurope.co.uk

*1. Shrike and Blessed Thistle*

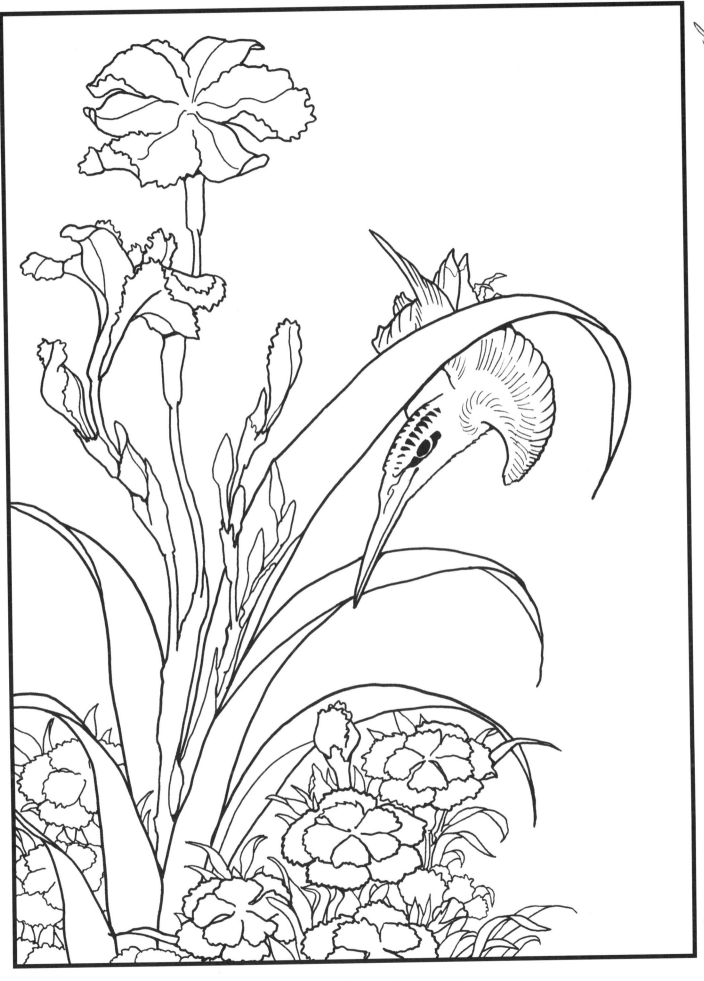

3. *Kingfisher with Iris and Wild Pinks*

5. Hawfinch and Marvel-of-Peru

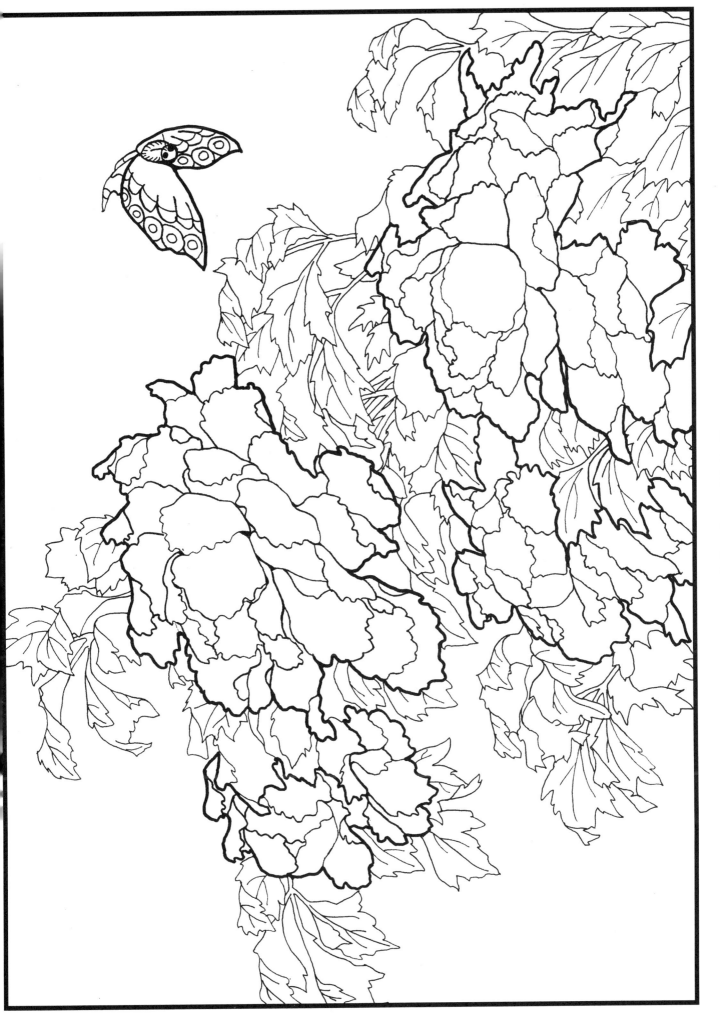

7. Peonies and Butterfly

*8. Shrike and Bluebird with Begonia and Wild Strawberry*

11. *Turtles and Reflected Plum Branch* (detail)

*12. Hawk and Cherry Blossoms* (detail)

13. *Java Sparrow on Magnolia*

*15. Bullfinch and Weeping Cherry*

16. Poppies

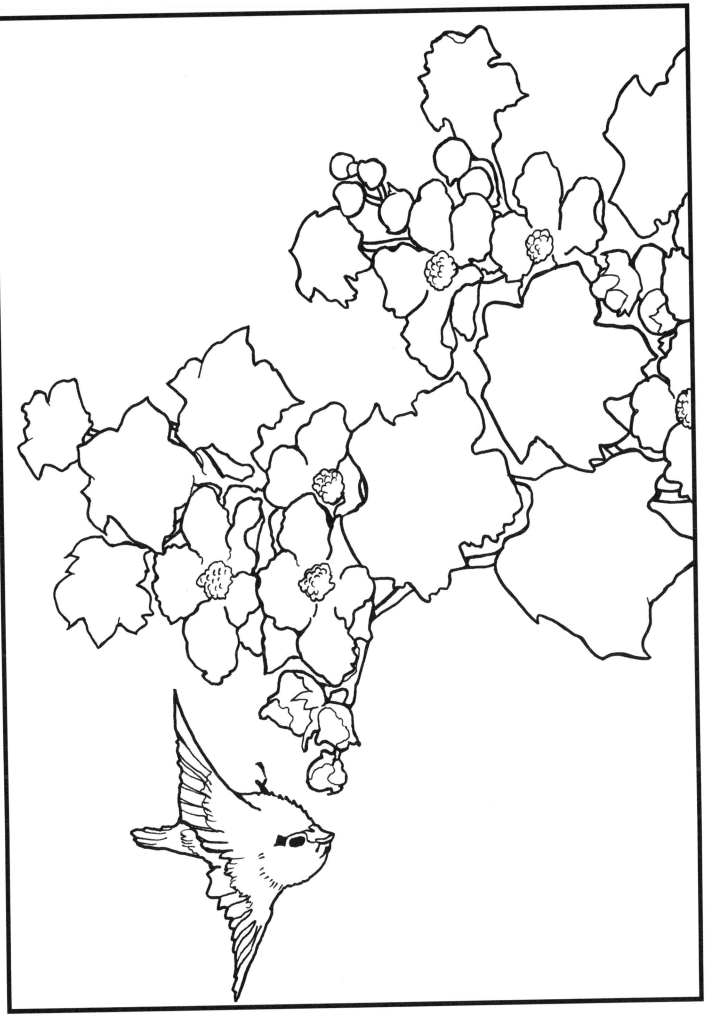

17. *Hibiscus and Sparrow*

*18. Warbler and Roses*

19. Bellflower and Dragonfly

20. *Wisteria and Wagtail*

21. Morning Glories and Tree Frog

22. Cuckoo and Azaleas

Draw and color your own picture here!